Jump in the Holes

*and other small ways
to live your biggest life*

Wendy Z Lewis

Jump in the Holes
Copyright © 2022 Wendy Z Lewis

Produced and printed by Stillwater River Publications.
All rights reserved. Written and produced in the United States of America.
This book may not be reproduced or sold in any form without the expressed,
written permission of the author and publisher.

Visit our website at
www.StillwaterPress.com
for more information.

First Stillwater River Publications Edition

ISBN: 978-1-955123-71-6

Library of Congress Control Number: 2021925246

1 2 3 4 5 6 7 8 9 10
Written by Wendy Z Lewis
Cover Design by Matthew St. Jean
Published by Stillwater River Publications,
Pawtucket, RI, USA.

Publisher's Cataloging-In-Publication Data
(Prepared by The Donohue Group, Inc.)
Names: Lewis, Wendy Z, author.
Title: Jump in the holes : and other small ways to
live your biggest life / Wendy Z Lewis.
Description: First Stillwater River Publications edition. |
Pawtucket, RI, USA : Stillwater River Publications, [2022]
Identifiers: ISBN 9781955123716
Subjects: LCSH: Inspiration--Humor. | Self-actualization
(Psychology)--Humor. | Conduct of life--Humor. |
LCGFT: Humor. | Essays.
Classification: LCC BF410 .L49 2022 |
DDC 153.3--dc23

JUMP IN THE HOLES

Contents

Preface

....

As a corporate copywriter, I was paid to tell other people's stories—stories that weren't particularly interesting. I spent my weekdays spinning tales about shingles vaccinations, 100% cotton tampons, and Easter candy.

Meanwhile, my own stories had been percolating in my brain—lessons about life, useful stuff I wanted to share with friends, and things I would teach my kids, if I had any (and if they would actually listen to me). When layoffs claimed my job and dysfunction ended my marriage, the ideas in my head began clamoring loudly, like attention-starved gremlins tugging at my pant leg. "Let us out!" they nagged. "Now you have time!"

I decided that my fiftieth year would be a fitting time to start sharing my stories because, by then, I was old enough to have weathered some of life's greatest challenges, yet still young enough to apply the wisdom I'd learned from their lessons. I began writing weekly essays called *Wendy Z Wednesdays* and publishing them in an online blog on (you guessed it) Wednesdays.

Jump in the Holes is the best of these essays, written between May 2019 and July 2020. The last three touch on the COVID-19 pandemic and racial unrest in 2020. Though these events hinge on particular dates and time periods, I've updated and included them because their teachings are timeless.

Life's lessons and gifts are all around each of us, every day. I hope these essays will inspire you to look for yours.

Jump in the Holes

*and other small ways
to live your biggest life*

....

Jump in the Holes

A better way to step through life

....

Six hundred bare feet paced around the room, faster and faster, following the rhythm of the hand drummers on the stage. I stomped along joyfully but cautiously, scanning the packed room.

I was one sweaty body in a crowd of about 300 who'd signed up for a weekend dance workshop at Omega Institute in Rhinebeck, New York, led by the late (and legendary) dance pioneer Gabrielle Roth. The course sessions were held in Omega's largest space, the Main Hall, but with so many people in attendance, it felt tight when all of those bodies started moving at the same time.

It seemed inevitable that people would soon start crashing into each other. "Go for the empty spaces," Roth said calmly through her microphone, and that seemed to make all the difference. My trajectory through the space had no plan. I chose my path moment by moment, each second moving my body wherever I saw a space that—for the moment anyway—was unoccupied by another body. I looked for the holes in the crowd and jumped in. If a space I was aiming for became occupied before I got to it, I simply changed direction; another hole would always open up somewhere else.

I saw others around me doing the same. We stole glimpses of each other's glowing smiles and ever-changing postures as we playfully bounced around. Sometimes mere inches separated us, but because we were all jumping in the holes, somehow all 300 of our strutting bodies managed to stay safe.

Roth's advice for navigating the dance floor so many years ago has stayed with me ever since, because it's great advice for navigating life in general. Whenever things feel too busy, too overwhelming or too staccato, I hear Roth's voice saying, "Go for the empty spaces," and I look for holes and jump in.

Beyond the dance floor, you can find—or create—holes whenever and wherever you need them; you can meditate for a few minutes in a quiet place, take a vacation from a busy job, breathe for a few moments in the car to clear your thoughts between appointments, or create a minimalist, serene corner at home.

The holes are the empty spaces in our days and lives where we can escape, regroup and refuel until we jump out again. They're like those "spaces between the notes" in music that Claude Debussy spoke of.* They're the little vacuums of "nothing" that help shape all the "everything" around them.

We need the holes. Without them, dancing bodies would collide, music would be noise, and our lives would be chaotic.

* *"Music is the space between the notes" is a quote often attributed to French composer Claude Debussy. I hope it's accurate.*

The Fucket List

It's the new bucket list.

....

You've probably heard of the bucket list—a list of all the things you'd like to do before you die. Bucket list items can be places you'd like to visit, goals you'd like to reach, and dreams you'd like to make come true.

Now, I'm a big believer in bucket lists (and goals, lists, and dreams in general). They help motivate us, sharpen our focus, and remind us to take the steps necessary to actually turn the stuff of our dreams into our reality. I have a bucket list. But I also have a fucket (or "Fuck It") list, and I add to it all the time.

The fucket list is my mental list of things I decide to no longer give a fuck about—a *To Don't* list, if you will. When I add things to my fucket list, I free myself from the mental burden of knowing they're still undone or unresolved.

For example, "speak Spanish fluently" was one of my bucket list items and, for a while, I became pretty damn good at speaking Spanish—not fluently, but good enough to carry on a simple conversation. (I have physical proof of this—a piece of artwork I bought from a little shop in Santo Domingo while on vacation several years ago. I negotiated the entire transaction *en Español!*) But since then, my Spanish skills have gotten *muy mal*. It really bothered me that I let my skills slip, until I realized that it's no failing of mine—life got busy and my priorities had to shift; that's just what priorities do. I can always return to Spanish. But for now, it's just not a big deal. I've put it on the fucket list, my mind is clearer for it, and I can still enjoy the artwork.

I added to my fucket list again recently when I came across a years-old bin of clothing I'd set aside to mend and alter. When I tried on the items, I found that some of them no longer needed altering, and others weren't even my style anymore. Rather than fret over the fact that I'd wasted the clothing, I moved some items to my "donate and bless someone else" pile, others to my "use the fabric to make something else" pile, and all of it, mentally, to my fucket list. It was freeing.

The fucket list is a great tool for a busy life. Whatever you consciously move to your fucket list will no longer have the power to make you feel guilty, angry or underproductive. You might still care about things on your fucket list, but they'll no longer drain your mental energy.

- House a mess? Move it to the fucket list.
- Job sucks? Fucket list.
- Still can't please your parents? Fucket list.
- Not yet a millionaire? Fucket list.
- Won't ever play classical guitar? Fucket list.
- May never be fluent in Japanese? Fucket list.

What worries you or constantly clutters your mind? All those undone "things to do," or maybe that family member who's never satisfied? Or those life goals you were brought up to believe you *had* to reach? Are they *really* that important, or are they just depleting your mental energy?

Bucket lists are great, but fucket lists are downright liberating. A fucket list allows you to shift your valuable focus, time, and effort forward—to future things that will feed your soul, better your life and help you be your best self.

Don't have a fucket list? Start one today.

In a Rut? Move That Butt.

The life-changing magic of asses and seats

....

Two college friends and I once caused a commotion when we did something crazy, rebellious and unexpected in class—we changed our seats.

You see, in this course—and just about every other course I took—on the first day, students would find a seat, and then gravitate to that *same* seat every day of the course thereafter. Not because the professor told them to. Not because the seats were assigned. But because, as humans, we tend to do stupid shit like stay within our comfort zones, operate on autopilot, get into routines and do what's easy.

It's important to note that this was a course related to psychology and interpersonal relationships, where we delved into the "whys" of human behavior. So, one afternoon when I had a study date with two friends from the class, we got into a discussion about the seating phenomenon. And then (geeky young rebels that we were), we decided we'd do a little behavior study of our own. The premise was simple—the next day of our class, we'd arrive early and sit separately, in seats our butts had never occupied before. We were curious how the other students would react, if they did at all.

Our little experiment created a bigger stir than we expected; when the other students arrived, they were visibly confused. Some even seemed a bit distressed or annoyed. But no one said anything, even those whose seats we had "taken," and they scrambled for other seats. It was a fairly small class with chairs arranged in a circle, so there wasn't anywhere to hide.

I exchanged glances with my friends as we watched everyone get settled. When our instructor (a very observant and eccentric old psychology buff) arrived and sat down, he looked around the circle, raised a bushy eyebrow at the three of us with a knowing smile, and began the class without a word.

After that day, my friends and I changed seats every session. Over time, the others seemed to grudgingly accept it while I found that I loved it. From different seats, I experienced the same class from different perspectives; each time, I noticed new things about the room, my classmates, and the course material.

That lesson wasn't in the curriculum, but its takeaways have stayed with me since:

- Change has the power to shift your perspective, both literally and figuratively.
- You don't have to wait for change; you can create your own.
- Change can be really upsetting or energizing— your choice.
- Even small changes can create a ripple effect—in ourselves and others.

Whenever I feel stuck, stagnated, or just plain bored with something, I remember that college class and then deliberately shift something in my physical world; I'll find a new spot in kickboxing class, declutter a drawer in my house, take a new path home or strike up a conversation with someone I don't usually speak with. Without fail, it seems to create a tiny mental and metaphysical shift that's just big enough to energetically push me out of that rut and onto a new path.

What rut are you in, and what tiny shift could you make— right now—to help get your ass out of it?

He's "FABULOUS!"

Paper, printer ink and life lessons—
all available at my local office supply store.

....

There was a guy who used to work the register at my local Staples. One of his legs was quite a bit shorter than the other, so one of his black orthopedic shoes had an extra-thick heel to make up for the difference in leg length. And he always wore the same pair of way-too-tight pants; one wrong move in those shoes and he could've easily split a seam. The first time I came to his checkout line he said, "How are you?"

"Fine, how are you?" I responded, focused more on fishing my wallet out of my purse than on how I was really doing. And to that he replied, "I'm FABULOUS!" with a booming voice, beaming smile and enthusiasm that came from the bottom of those shoes, reverberated in his whole body (and those too-tight pants) and embodied the word "fabulous" with a verve that made me bust into a smile, too. This guy meant it, and his energy was contagious.

During every visit to the store, when I went through his checkout, our exchange was always the same. And I started looking forward to hearing him say, "Fabulous!" Some people may have looked at him and thought that, as a wardrobe- and height-challenged clerk working in an office supply store, he had nothing much to feel fabulous about. But *he* knew he did. I never learned his back story, but he was obviously someone who focused on the positive things in his life rather than the negatives. And in doing so, his enthusiasm always spilled across the counter like a wave of happiness and made me feel just a little sheepish for not doing the same.

Years later, I still remember his booming voice, and I'm reminded to appreciate all the things in *my* life that are "fabulous!" and not just "fine."

May you have a "FABULOUS!" day.

That Time I Watched
a Bug Get Naked

....

One of the most memorable things about being a kid in Queens, New York was the roar of the cicadas in late summer. Young cicadas would shed their juvenile exoskeletons on the trees to begin their next phase of life as winged adults. They'd fly off to sing for mates—their scratchy mating songs punctuating the summer evenings, their old beige skins abandoned on the trees of my block.

My best friend's brother collected the exoskeletons; each day finding a few more on the trees, picking them carefully off the bark and adding them to the ever-growing stash of hollow cicada skins he kept in Dixie cups in his bedroom (gross, I know—but that's what kids do). Some were missing a leg or two, some were frozen in funny poses that my friend and I would imitate, but each brittle, transparent shell shared the same distinctive feature—a neat split at the shoulders—its former occupant's exit door from its old life.

As a child, I saw an occasional live cicada on the sidewalk, likely suffering from the unforgiving concrete heat—either ambling slowly as if in a daze, or circling on its back, white belly up, frantically beating its wings and rattling abrasively with the incessant buzz of a tiny electric razor. But usually, it was their empty shells I saw—hundreds of them, dappling the trees like little transparent spacesuits discarded by tiny aliens, their owners long departed, hooked feet still clinging to the bark.

Though I saw the shells everywhere, I never actually saw a cicada squeeze out of one—not until I was about 25. I was at my then-boyfriend's house. It was early evening and dusk was falling. I forget why I was walking through their

9

backyard alone, but that's what I was doing, when I almost walked into it—a solitary cicada, at eye level on a tree, just beginning its tight squeeze from its shell. I stood, transfixed. My boyfriend's mom called for me—dinner was ready—but I wouldn't come in. My boyfriend called me too, and then his dad, but no, I'd never seen this before and damn it, I was going to watch it.

The tiny dramatic struggle began to play out in front of me—the adult cicada quietly emerging, slowly and painstakingly, damp, naked, and vulnerable, sharing its rite of passage only with me—a lucky audience of one. I yelled for the others to come out and watch, but they just laughed at me, the crazy girl watching a bug in the backyard.

It took about 20 minutes for the clumsy creature with the bulging eyes to finally free himself completely. When he did, he climbed up on his former skin on new, tiny legs and perched at the split as if he'd reached a mountain summit, slowly fanning his wings in triumph. I'd always found the cicadas creepy and ugly, but its transformation had been surprisingly beautiful. I was teased throughout dinner, but no one could dampen my joy; I knew I'd witnessed something precious—a fellow earth creature's life passage—and the others had missed it. Their loss.

That cicada is long gone, but it taught me to look for the tiny, beautiful dramas that are surely playing out all around us, all the time. How many moments do we miss when we are rushing off to dinner or whatever else is so damn important?

Always make time for the unexpected surprises that pop up in front of you; they're The Universe's little gifts, just for you. Dinner can wait.

Touchdown at a
Fake Super Bowl

....

When the New England Patriots scored the touchdown and won the game, I leaped off the sofa, screaming, fists overhead. My husband high-fived our kids, a boy and girl ages six and nine, who were also yelling and cheering. My heart pumped and my adrenaline soared. Faces flushed, we all sat back down on the sofa and calmed ourselves. Then we did it again. And once more. Then the director stopped the camera and thanked us before we all filed calmly out of the room.

You see, it wasn't a real football game; it was an audition for a TV commercial in a casting agency office in Boston. I'd just met the guy and children who were supposedly my husband and kids, and the director had coached us through the entire scenario: "You're watching the Super Bowl on TV in your living room. The Patriots are one touchdown away from winning. It's been a white-knuckled, edge-of-your-seat game the whole way through. I want to see the anticipation on your faces when you're not sure if they're going to score, and then when I wave my hand, you see the touchdown, and you react!"

After the audition, I took the elevator down to the first floor of the high-rise office building with my fake son and his real dad. I waved an enthusiastic goodbye to them and practically skipped to my car. The thing was, although that adrenaline-flushed, victorious football moment had been completely fabricated (and I'm not even a football fan), my body didn't know the difference. I sat for a moment in my car, completely pumped, amazed and amused at how I felt—like I could accomplish anything, do anything—the rest of the day, and in my life in general. And it got me thinking.

Often, we believe we have to get motivated before we can take action. But actually, the reverse also works—we can take action that motivates us and *then* accomplish what we want to do. Before the audition, I knew of famous and not-so-famous people (like Tony Robbins, David Goggins and my martial arts instructor) who swore by their "get motivated" routines—fist pumps, deep breathing, cold morning showers and more—to get their bodies and minds primed for productivity and high performance. But it wasn't until I experienced it myself that I truly understood how well it works. I don't yet have a special routine of my own, but I've found that sometimes just launching myself into a project—even one that I dread—creates motivation along the way.

And no, I didn't get the commercial, but I got a great lesson. Touchdown!

It's Not Your Intuition

....

There's a powerful opening chapter in Gavin de Becker's book *The Gift of Fear** where the author interviews a brave survivor of a rape and attempted murder. After a male stranger sweet-talked his way into the woman's apartment, she somehow knew that despite his assurances, her attacker intended to murder her. She then smoothly escaped the apartment, found refuge in a neighbor's apartment, and escaped death. And she did it all using her intuition—or did she?

De Becker spoke with her and slowly recounted the events, step by painful step. She realized that, although she had no survival training, nor had ever encountered such a situation before, a lifetime of reading subtle social cues gave her the information she needed to save her life. How did she know he intended to kill her violently, even though he promised her he wouldn't? *Because he closed the window and turned up the music.* How did she know he was going to get a weapon? *Because he headed down the hallway toward the kitchen—and the knives.* How did she know she could slip into her neighbor's apartment? *Because they always left their door unlocked.*

In New Age circles, I often hear people say, "Well, maybe it's just my intuition, but I knew ... " As in, "Maybe it was just my intuition, but I knew she was upset with me." *Of course you knew ... she stopped accepting your lunch invitations.* Or "It must've been my intuition—I knew their marriage was in trouble!" *Yeah, she complained about him pretty often.* That's not intuition. Don't get me wrong; intuition does exist, and things can happen on an energetic level that we often can't explain. That's not what I'm talking about.

What's not our "intuition" are things that we know because—if you really stop and think them through—there

13

were so many cues, clues and hints that Ray Charles could've seen them.

So why do we credit our "intuition?" Because we want to feel special. Or maybe because we want a little magic in our lives—a departure from our everyday routines and average days. And that's understandable. There's a difference between information that's actually psychic/intuitive and the information we receive as part of the innate survival gift we've all been given. This gift is the ability to read and give heed to the often-subtle verbal and nonverbal cues that are always there as we navigate our interactions with others every single day. They're so subtle and omnipresent that they tend to fade into the background of our day, like beige wallpaper, until we really reflect.

If—when you really think it through—you can explain why you "knew" something, it wasn't your intuition. But that doesn't make you any less special; you were just using a different set of skills.

* The Gift of Fear: And Other Survival Signals That Protect Us from Violence *is a fascinating book by Gavin de Becker, a security specialist and expert on the prediction and management of violence.*

Sometimes It's Great When Things Suck. Here's Why.

....

Recently, I ran into a friend whom I hadn't seen in months. "How're you doing?" I asked. After a long pause and a serious look, she finally replied. "Actually, things kind of suck right now. I'm not doing too well."

I loved her honesty.

Maybe like me, you've heard about positive thinking; how you can bring great things into your life by changing your negative thoughts and words to positive ones. Stuff like, "Expect a miracle today!" or "Act like everything's great, and it will be!"

There's a lot to positive thinking. Our thoughts, words, and actions have a huge impact on how we experience daily life. But I've literally seen people force out "Everything is going great!" through gritted teeth or tight smiles, or start stressing and obsessing over whether their thoughts and words were "positive enough." That's why I admired my friend so much for being brutally honest—to me and herself.

Every day I give thanks for all the things I have that many people in this world do not. I have my health and the ability to see, hear, touch, taste and smell. And I enjoy abundance—I have food in the kitchen, a car to drive, and marketable skills. And I was born to responsible parents, in an area of the world where I enjoy freedoms many people don't. And I have friends and family who care about me. All these things are priceless, and I am fortunate.

You may have similar blessings in your life, yet I'll bet that sometimes things still feel sucky. You may suffer from small daily annoyances like losing your keys again when you are already 10 minutes late, or big crappy problems like losing your job. No matter how blessed we know we are or how badly others throughout the world are struggling, there are times we are just not feeling it.

That's why I think sometimes it can be healthy to step back from the feel-good positivity parade and acknowledge the Suck Factor. Why? Because it can be a powerful trigger for change.

It's impossible to change something until you acknowledge that *something is wrong*. The trick is to wallow in the bad feelings—a little. Not so much that you want to find a bridge to jump from, but just enough that you can say to yourself, *Yes, this thing sucks.* Then identify exactly what about it sucks, and why. And what you can do to change it so it doesn't suck anymore.

Doctors say that pain is the body's way of telling us something's wrong; it's how we know we have an infection or an injury and can then take steps to heal it. In a similar way, feelings of sadness, anger, dissatisfaction, restlessness, frustration and more can tell us what needs special attention in our lives—if we listen.

Regreats

....

I've regretted doing—and not doing—lots of things in my life. For example, I shouldn't have stayed in some relationships or toxic jobs as long as I did. I also shouldn't have wasted good money on a few stupid things. I definitely should've bought Amazon stock back in 1997. Those are some of my regrets, and I'm sure you have yours, too.

But recently, I heard something that made me reframe my regrets in a whole new way—in a grab-my-phone-and-dictate-that-into-my-notes kind of way. In a *YouTube* video about productive morning routines, entrepreneur Tom Bilyeu* casually threw out a gem of wisdom: if you aren't embarrassed by who you were a year ago, then you aren't growing.

Wow. Think about that for a second. It means that having regrets is *good*. If you can look back on something in your life and think, "What the hell was I thinking?" it's proof that you have grown since then and you know better now. The real tragedy would be to reflect on where you were one year, five years, or 10 years ago, say, "Yeah, cool," and go right on thinking and doing all the same things today.

Do you have regrets? That's great! Because it means you're constantly improving—getting better, smarter and more kickass every year. It also means you can go ahead and forgive your younger self. In fact, you can thank "the old you" for teaching "the new you" something.

I propose that we start calling regrets "regreats." Because the lessons we learned the last time will help us be great the next time.

* *Tom Bilyeu is an American entrepreneur and all-around badass best known as co-founder of Quest Nutrition and CEO of Impact Theory, a weekly online interview show that explores the success secrets of some of the world's highest achievers.*

Red, White, and Blue— and an Independent You

....

Independence Day in the United States is a federal holiday commemorating the thirteen original colonies' secession from Great Britain in 1776.

It's also a time when, every year, I reflect on my personal independence. Just as the leaders of the thirteen colonies said, "Fuck 'em! We don't need them anymore! We'd be better off without them,"* at this time each year, I reflect on the things in my life I've liberated myself from and consider what else might go.

In the last few years, I've eliminated:

- Cable TV and TV altogether (I don't own one).
- Two-thirds of my book collection.
- A toxic marriage.
- A toxic job.
- A ridiculously large house.
- Unsupportive "friends."
- Excessive time wasters (like Facebook—I now limit my daily usage).
- Unused subscriptions to magazines, entertainment and services.

Currently, I'm working on eliminating unnecessary things from my new living space—mainly clothes and household items. I'm not exactly a minimalist, but the idea inspires me. With less of the wrong things, I am more right with myself.

On July Fourth, let the parades, flags and festivities inspire you to create your own personal declaration of independence from whatever in your life is not serving you. Your fireworks will shine brighter without them.

* My historical knowledge stinks. Maybe none of them literally said that, but I think that captures the general idea.

What Hikers Can Teach Us About Making Decisions

....

I've heard that if you get lost in the woods, you can find your way to your destination once you find True North. Though I'm not much of a hiker or backpacker, this principle has served me well when navigating some of life's most demanding journeys.

It's much easier to travel a treacherous path when you've established your "True North"—that is, what's most important to you, at that time, in that situation. For example, when I was navigating my divorce, I decided that my True North would be, "Get out as quickly as I can, with as little emotional pain as possible." Every mile I traveled along the long path to divorce, there were many decisions to be made, uncomfortable situations to be navigated, and lots of work to be done. Through it all, my True North was my guide, helping me stay true to my course in moments of confusion until I reached my final destination of singlehood and peace.

Had my True North been "Save all the money I can," or "Get revenge!" I would have made different adjustments along my journey. Likewise, five other people in a similar situation would choose five unique paths, and each person's True North would honor what's most important to them.

If you've found yourself deep in the woods of a life situation, get still and figure out your True North. It will help you stay on the right trails and find your way home.

When You Don't Belong and You Don't Know Why

....

I once trained in a Brazilian martial art called Capoeira. I'd read about it for years and wanted to learn more but there just aren't that many Capoeira schools in the United States. So, when I moved to a new state, imagine my excitement when I learned that there was a Capoeira school just miles from my new home!

After I moved, I checked out the school, signed up, and started regular classes. I loved Capoeira and I loved the school. The only problem was, the people in the school didn't seem to love *me*. Now, no one was outwardly rude or unwelcoming and I actually did make a few acquaintances there. But somehow, from my first class to my last (a year and a half later), I just didn't ever seem to really be a *part* of things.

I went to classes regularly. I talked to people. And I put in lots of effort to develop my Capoeira skills and my relationships with my classmates, but nothing really seemed to change; I wasn't given the level of instruction I'd paid for (while younger students were), wasn't notified of special workshops I would have been interested in, and was regularly passed over for awards and recognition newer students received. It felt like a high school clique in which I would never be accepted.

I spent a lot of time wondering why things felt that way and what I might do to change it. Was it that I was "too old?" (After all, I was a near-geriatric 34 at the time, while most of the other students were college aged.) Was I "too American?" (Most of the students were Brazilian or Cape Verdean.) Was I "too unavailable?" (I had a steady boyfriend outside the school, while there were many active student/student and student/teacher romances.)

The last straw was when I asked the school owner/my instructor why he'd passed me over for my first promotion when I'd clearly exceeded all the criteria.

His reply: I hadn't yet been training for the minimum required eight months. That's when it became clear that, in the *eighteen* months I'd busted my ass training there, he'd never noticed. That's when it also became clear that I was wasting my time and money. So I left.

I never figured out what the deal was at the Capoeira school, but it doesn't matter. Because when I stopped trying to fit in there, I was able to focus my energy elsewhere in my new home state. And that was when I found tons of friends and other social groups where the people were welcoming and valued what I had to offer. And yes, that included a different martial arts school where I started training in another art I liked even more than Capoeira.

Every one of us feels like an outsider sometimes—at a party, at a new job, or when you're trying out Zumba and you're the only one who doesn't know the steps. Sometimes it'll take a few minutes or days to feel like you fit in, and other times—like at my Capoeira school—it'll just never happen at all. And you know what? If it doesn't, that's okay. Fuck 'em. It's not you. Your tribe exists, just not there. Move on and find it; they're waiting for you.

Where Was That Wormhole?

*One theory for why time moves faster
as you get older, and how to slow it down*

....

When I was younger (a lot younger), I remember older people saying how time passes faster as you get older. That seemed strange—after all, time is a defined quantity, right? One second—or minute or month or year—passes the same for one person as it does the next.

But then, somewhere around my mid-thirties, there was a strange shift. I'd remember a friend's birthday, a trip, or some other event, and think it happened a few months ago. Then, when I talked to the friend or looked at my calendar, I'd realize it actually happened a year ago. Or two. Or five. I'd wonder, *Where did the time go? Did I pass through a wormhole somewhere, like space-time travelers did on Star Trek?* And then I'd think, *Oh crap, I sound old.*

When we haven't lived too many years, the ones we have lived have more significance. But once we've lived long enough to get decades of birthdays and some major life events under our belts, we get so accustomed to the whole "living your life" thing that each passing day, week, month—and year—seems to mean less. I think that's one of the reasons why time seems to pass faster as we get older.

But no matter how many years we've lived, we can amp up our awareness and appreciation for each passing moment, essentially slowing down the passage of time once again. And actually, I would propose that the older we get, the better we should be able to slow down time, because the more days we've lived, the more appreciation we have for each of them, and the more awareness we have for what we might accomplish tomorrow.

No, maybe we can't literally expand time. But we can come pretty damn close if we change the way we experience the time we have left.

The Void of Joy

....

There's a lot of talk in New Age-y circles about gratitude—that is, acknowledging and being thankful for the things you have. Studies have shown that people who regularly practice gratitude are happier, nicer to others, and physically healthier than their non-thankful "Negative Nelly" counterparts.

Those who practice gratitude acknowledge the importance of giving thanks not just for "big" things like new cars, job promotions, or unexpected checks in the mail, but also the small, everyday delights like a delicious cookie, a call from a friend, or the sound of birds singing.

Daily, I give thanks for all those things too, but I also include a third, often overlooked category: the shit I *don't* have.

For example, today I'm thankful that:

- The temperature in my house is comfortable because I don't have a broken HVAC system.
- I was able to spend the day being productive and happy (not in panic mode) because I did not lose my cell phone.
- I don't have heartache because I ended that weird, red-flag-riddled relationship early.

"Lack" is a word that usually describes a negative, like a lack of food, money, or time. But I like to extend that good 'ol gratitude to include lack—the lack of negatives that would hamper my capacity to celebrate the positives.

In short, I acknowledge the peace and joy that certain kinds of "lack" bring. Sure, having gratitude for positive things is great. But don't overlook The Lack of Bad. Because then you realize that most days—even those without singing birds, pastel sunrises, and hugs from strangers—are actually pretty damn good.

Their Success Doesn't
Mean You're a Failure

....

Just about every self-awareness and spirituality guru has something that they promise will *change your life*. (And they will let you in on that secret for just three easy payments of $599.) Today, I'd like to share—for free—something that truly changed my life, and maybe it will yours, too.

We all want things in life. For most of us, it's probably one or more of these:

- A great body.
- A great relationship.
- Satisfying work.
- Lots of money.

Most of us make it to adulthood wanting these (or similar) things, and feeling jealous when others—people we know, people on TV, people we read about—get those things, while we sit there, feeling the definite *lack* of those things and feeling jealous, envious and massively pissed off that they have it and we don't. So basically, you set yourself up to feel crappy whenever something good happens to anyone. That's what happens when you have a scarcity mentality.

With a **scarcity mentality**, your outlook is, "There's only so much to go around; if someone else has what I want, there's that much less for me."

If you have a scarcity outlook you may tend to say whiny, pouty things like, "Wow, must be nice to have that," or "Some people have all the luck." You may come away from an interaction with some doesn't-deserve-it fuckface feeling like a deflated failure. (And the other person will probably come away thinking, "Wow, what a jerk.")

So, what's the solution? Shift to an **abundance mentality**. An outlook of abundance says, "There's plenty more where that came from; if someone else got what I want, it's proof that it can happen for me, too."

Why do we get ourselves in such a bind, and make ourselves feel terrible in the process? Because we're assuming that The Universe (or the laws of science, or Spirit, or God, or Allah, or The Happy Unicorn of Life—whatever force you believe governs the way things work) works the way we humans do. For example, if we only have 10 dollars, and we spend eight on lunch, then we *only have* two more. If we work nine hours a day and sleep for another seven, then we *only have* eight more hours in our 24-hour day to do the things we really want to do. We're used to thinking in finite terms.

But The Universe (or whatever you want to call it) doesn't work that way; it's as easy for The Big U to create a mountain as it is to create a grain of sand, or to bestow a million dollars on a million people instead of just one.

I don't understand exactly how it all works,* but I do know that shifting your perspective to one of abundance can make you a much happier person, open to all the possibilities of abundance coming your way. I know because it worked for me. An abundance mentality frees you of jealousy and allows you to be truly happy for others. It also helps you get pumped up by others' good fortune and see everything that happens to them as proof that your dreams can—and will—be supported too.

But if you're a curious person who must know exactly how all of this works, there are a ton of books, YouTube videos and TED Talks on metaphysics that you can explore. Let me know what you learn.

I'll Take Those Problems, Please

You will have challenges. Choose your favorites.

....

Problems are inevitable; they're a part of life. No matter where we were born or what situation we were born into, we will always have "problems," "challenges," "concerns" or whatever you'd like to call "shit in life that sucks." In fact, some spiritual folks believe that problems are actually central to our physical experience on earth at this time, on this plane of existence in time and space.

The only thing that may differ from person to person is *which* problems they experience. While some problems are beyond our control, a great many of them end up being ours based on which life paths we choose. For example:

- A nine-to-five corporate worker chose the security of a steady paycheck but hates the boredom of his daily routine; a small business owner loves his freedom of schedule but complains about unsteady income.
- A mom of six always wanted a big family but feels like she has no time to herself; a single woman loves her independence but feels lonely on the weekends.
- A married man loves having a wife and family but hates Sundays with the in-laws; a single man loves dating different women but fears he'll die alone.
- A garage band guitarist is passionate about his music but hates playing the local dive bars; his famous idol loves his financial success but hates spending months away from his family when he's touring.

- A homeowner loves the stability of knowing she has a secure place to live but hates the maintenance and upkeep; a renter loves having the landlord fix things but hates knowing he could be kicked out when his lease is up.

It's like you're in the Cafeteria of Life, picking a little of this and a bit of that and adding it to your tray; the spicy curry would be delicious but may later give you heartburn, and the salad may be healthy but will leave green things in your teeth. No choice is necessarily good or bad, but each comes with its own unique side dish of challenges. (Some people call this "choosing your shit sandwich" but since we're speaking metaphorically, we can leave that unappetizing item off the menu entirely.)

Since you will always have problems in life, it's pointless to try and have none, and then get all whiny when they pop up. Instead, embrace the fact that problems will come, and consider *which set of problems* you'd rather deal with. The problems you are more willing to have will help you make wise choices and prevent future regrets.

Every choice and every life path brings its own unique set of problems. Which will you choose?

Wait a Minute

A Zen approach to long lines, traffic
jams and other time vampires

....

Whoever said, "Patience is a virtue" never got stuck in traffic. There is something uniquely aggravating about being forced to a crawl when you're on the run. Traffic and road rage are proof of that, as are things like slow checkout lines, slow WiFi connections and slow walkers in narrow aisles.

The one good thing about being forced to move at tortoise speed while in hare mode is that at least we can control how we react. I once got stuck in a huge traffic jam on the highway in pouring rain. Cars were barely crawling along and, in the downpour, I couldn't see what was causing the car constipation or where the blockage might end. I decided then that I could either be pissed off or make the most of the moment. I was dry and safe, so I figured I was already a lot better off than whoever might have had an accident up ahead. So I decided to throw a traffic jam celebration.

I put on a party song, turned it up loud and, instead of screaming about the delay, I belted out the lyrics, dancing in my seat. Before the first song was halfway through, I realized I was having a hell of a great time. Even better, I lifted the spirits of a senior couple in another car who'd seen my little party through the foggy window and pulled up beside me, smiling and shyly waving.

I think of that rainy day whenever I'm stuck somewhere I didn't plan to be. Instead of getting annoyed, I try to welcome those moments as opportunities to breathe and get centered, especially when I haven't been meditating like I should. I like to think The Universe is giving me those moments to help me out because I didn't make that time for myself in the first place. Or maybe The Big U is holding me up a bit so I don't rush into that busy intersection and get hit by that crazy driver.

Of course, it's easier to be Zen about it when I'm not pressed for time, but I've found that viewing those annoying little "waits" as opportunities has made them a lot less aggravating. Plus, those small moments are great practice for life's bigger moments, when the shit's really hitting the fan.

No one likes waiting, but sometimes those slowdowns are the only waking moments we have in our day for stillness. Your next wait—whether it's a few seconds at a crosswalk or 20 minutes in traffic—isn't time wasted if you use it well.

How could you better use your next delay? Practice deep breathing. Smile at or chat with the person next to you (as long as you don't complain about the wait). Or use the time to really *notice* something around you, even if you've been there many times before. Resist the urge to pull out your phone.

Slowdowns will happen. Will you use yours for road rage or a car party? It's your choice.

Fear is a Faker

Fear can save us or stunt us.
When should we ignore it?

....

We humans are hard-wired with many gifts, and one of the most useful is fear. Sometimes it shows up as that sharp, can't-deny-it knot in the gut that keeps us from walking down a particular dark alley. Other times it's a quiet, persistent unease that gnaws away at us until we reconsider doing something stupid. It's pretty handy.

Unfortunately, fear can also be a sniveling little coward who stands on your foot, preventing you from taking steps toward greatness. Fear often entices us to stay in our comfort zones, where everything is nice and cozy but we aren't challenged to expand. So sometimes we must suck up our discomfort, feel a little fear, and do that thing we dread. Now, I am not recommending that you give fear the middle finger and go jogging through Central Park at 3 a.m. But recognize that there are times when you should tell fear to shut up and crawl under a rock until you really need it.

There are two kinds of fear: the useful, intuitive kind that can save your life and the self-sabotaging kind that can keep you from achieving some great shit in your life. Sometimes, it's hard to know the difference.

In my life, I didn't do many things I should have because of stupid, self-sabotaging fear (like not leveraging a job in my 20s that could have jump-started my career). Conversely, I've done other things even though I was scared shitless (like fight a six-foot-tall male black belt in a martial arts tournament).

So I've learned to ask myself some questions that help me discern between real fear and bullshit fear. Maybe they'll help you, too:

Will I regret not doing this?

Travel forward in time one year, five years, maybe to the end of your life. Is there a chance that good things could come from this at a later time? Could this be a good learning opportunity? Projecting yourself into the future puts you in a more relaxed, less "everything hinges on this" mental place from where you can think more clearly.

How loud are the voices in my head?

The voices we most need to hear are often the quietest. Our intuition often speaks in fleeting whispers, easily drowned out by our louder, inner voice of self-doubt. Either can be ignored.

Am I rationalizing?

Here's an interesting irony: often, when there's something scary we know we should do, we rationalize all the reasons why we shouldn't. We tell ourselves things like, "I can't take that job—it's over my head." But when our gut is trying to tell us not to do something, we rationalize reasons why we should, for example: "I know you're not supposed to accept rides from strangers, but he's well-dressed and anyway, I don't want to be rude." Listen to your internal dialogue—it may provide clues that reveal what kind of fear you're feeling.

Once we get better at recognizing "fake fear," we can let it stop sabotaging our lives. Because sometimes the things we think we're afraid to do are actually the things we most need to do. Though it can be hard to get comfortable with feeling uncomfortable, it gets easier with practice.

A shy friend of mine once volunteered to work on a political campaign so she would be forced to go door-to-door and talk to people. It was a win-win; she built her social confidence while helping a cause she believed in. In the same way, taking bigger and bigger steps out of your "comfort bubble" can help get you started on the path to your best life.

So if your fear is fake, tell it to shut up. Then tell that cute guy or girl you really, really like them. Or, tell your boss it's time for that raise. Or, tell your travel agent that yes, you're finally booking that dream trip. And then tell yourself you totally rock.

The Tao of Decluttering

Bruce Lee and the art of throwing shit out

....

Piles, piles all around—pictures, letters, cards, and mementos—what to keep and what to toss? I've been on a minimizing/decluttering kick after I downsized from my marriage and gigantic house to singlehood and a smaller house. One moving truck, two dumpsters and countless hours of sweat equity later, I'm really digging a more minimalist way of life. While it's been challenging to "Marie Kondo" my way through piles of clothes, books, and all those other things that seem to breed like wild rabbits while my back is turned, it's nothing compared to minimizing sentimental stuff.

Last weekend I leaped over a nostalgic hurdle; I went through a large bin of paper—letters, cards, and some photos—that I'd been accumulating for decades. It was an eclectic party of items, some of it dating back more than 20 years: batches of airmail letters from long-lost pen pals; anniversary cards from old boyfriends; several 30th birthday cards from a close friend; handwritten letters and Christmas cards from my long-passed paternal grandparents; and letters those grandparents wrote to each other in 1937 during their engagement (32 years before I was even born).

Yes, open space (and less stuff cluttering it up) is my goal, but at what price? I admire the modern-day minimalist nomads who couchsurf, work remotely from coffee shops, and hop continents, carrying everything they own in a backpack or two. In their quest to minimize, however, they are forced to keep only what's most utilitarian. It's a lifestyle that doesn't allow much room for pieces of personal history—the reminders of who and what has brought vibrancy, color and uniqueness to life's journey.

As I sorted items into piles and wondered what to do with all of it, I was reminded of a philosophy of Bruce Lee (a man I admire for many reasons): "Absorb what is useful, reject what is useless and add what is essentially your own."* I've applied it to my martial arts training, life wisdom, and people, so I decided I'd also apply it to the items in the bin. Letters from long-lost pen pals, boyfriends and "friends" who wronged me? Gone. Cards and letters from dear, still-in-my-life friends? Keep. My grandparents' engagement letters? Add acid-free sleeves and store with great care.

My new house is a delicious combination of new things and old, in a space that's growing less cluttered all the time. The cherished older things seem to radiate in the new space as if they know they've made the cut—proud reminders of my history and staunch supporters of my future.

When we clear out what we no longer need, we create space in our homes, lives and minds for the objects, people and ideas that will serve us best going forward. Bruce Lee was right about many things, but especially this.

On the inside cover of Lee's Tao of Jeet Kune Do, *he dedicates the book " . . . to the free, creative martial artist: research your own experience; absorb what is useful, reject what is useless and add what is essentially your own."*

The Power of Through

Sometimes it's the only way. And that's okay.

....

I love GPS navigation. It's especially novel when you're old enough to remember driving around with maps. (Remember those spiral-bound map books where you had to flip pages to see your whole trip?) GPS already knows your start point. You just input an end point, tap "Go" and (*poof!*) your best route to your destination magically appears, usually with one or two alternates if you want to avoid tolls or take the scenic route.

Unfortunately, there's no GPS for some of life's most difficult trips. Sometimes, you just have to get from Point A (where you are now) to Point B (where you want to be) without a Magic GPS Life Fairy to suggest alternate ways around the figurative tolls, potholes, traffic jams, or accidents you'll surely encounter along the way.

When I was facing divorce, I dreaded what I'd heard is a long, torturous process that's about as much fun as a root canal. It was then that a friend (who'd been through it herself) told me, "Sometimes, the only way out is through." So I gritted my teeth and set out on what I knew would be a marathon of sorts. To break up the long journey, I set smaller goals along the way—like the mile markers at real marathons—so I'd be able to measure my progress and know that eventually I would reach my destination, no matter how far away it often seemed.

When I'd checked the last goal off my list ("Sell the marital home"), I knew I'd crossed the finish line. It was a quiet victory; at the closing, there was no one to clap, hand me Gatorade, take a picture, or put a medal around my neck (though my real estate agent gave me a quick hug before saying goodbye). But gratification came from knowing that I had been transformed from my journey *through*—growth and change that I would have missed had I been able to choose an alternate route.

Recently, I tried a vigorous hot yoga class at a new studio. When I opened the door and my body hit the wall of 90-plus-degree steamy heat, it reacted with a near-primal *"What the fuck?"* and then, *"Why are we doing this?"* It was a tangible reminder that the process *is* the transformation, and sometimes there are no shortcuts. "We need this," I told my body. "When we leave, our muscles will be relaxed and the aches will be gone. We'll be renewed, as if we've been baptized in our own sweat." As I unrolled my mat and plunked my ass down on it, I remembered my friend's wise words for divorce and life in general: "Sometimes, the only way out is through."

Gray Decisions and the 30% Rule

The hardest choices aren't black and white.

....

Some decisions are pretty easy to make. Growing up, most of us honed our decision-making skills with easy stuff like, *Should I wear the blue pants or the brown ones? Should I sit here or there on the school bus?*

But no amount of practice really prepares us for the realities of adulthood, where sometimes we're whomped over the head with what I call "Gray Decisions." That is, those tough-as-hell quandaries that aren't nearly as clear-cut as, *Should I get the small coffee or the large?* Nope, not that easy. Gray Decisions are those smoky, slippery, intangible dilemmas like, *Should I stay in this marriage? Should I move across the country? Should I take that job?*

Gray Decisions are often characterized by one or more of the following:

- We don't have enough information to truly compare our options.
- We do have all the information we need, but something still feels "off."
- There are multiple possible outcomes, not just "this or that."
- Our decision will affect loved ones.
- Our options are as different as apples and oranges—with a few pears and bananas thrown in, just to make it more interesting.

Gray Decisions can render us immobile, unable to decide on a course of action while we analyze all the possibilities to death. It's like we're standing next to a tree, our hands on the trunk and our eyes tracing all the possible paths up from each branch to the hundreds of possible twigs and leaves; the starting point is the same, but the end points are all unique. How do you choose?

When I faced a Gray Decision a few years ago, a good friend of mine told me something very profound. Easy decisions, he said, are one hundred percent "yes" and zero percent "no." Even decisions of ninety to eighty percent "yes" and ten to twenty percent "no" are still pretty easy, but the tipping point, he said, is around seventy/thirty. Even though seventy is a pretty big "yes" number, it's that dang thirty percent "no" that can really get your pants in a bind. That thirty percent (or more) is what causes even the most level-headed people to do a ton of hemming and hawing, head-scratching and handwringing.

That thirty percent is where all the "buts" live. As in, *Moving to a lower-cost state makes the most financial sense but I'll miss all my friends.* Or, *Being free of that relationship will give me peace of mind, but where will I live?* Gray Decisions aren't black or white, but a blend of the two; they're a shade of gray—a maddening blend of "yes" and "no." And my friend's "thirty percent rule" means that any decision with a "no" factor of thirty percent or more is going to cause you lots of headaches.

When I was making that Gray Decision, I often thought of a passage from *The Bell Jar* by Sylvia Plath, where she described her many life options as figs on a tree that eventually dried up and fell to the ground because she took too long to choose one.* Like Plath, I also suffered from "analysis paralysis" but ultimately, I had to choose the best path I could envision. No, my decision wasn't black and white, or one hundred percent/ zero percent. It was around the seventy/thirty tipping point that my wise friend described; that seventy percent "yes" made it clear what to do, but the thirty percent "no" made it hard to actually do it. But the farther I got down the branch of my decision, the easier the path became. And, looking back at the trunk, I know I chose wisely.

* Check out a hauntingly beautiful rendition of the "figs" passage by comic artist Gavin Aung Than on zenpencils.com: https://www.zenpencils.com/comic/130-sylvia-plath-the-fig-tree/

If Your Memory Sucks,
Don't Fret It—Just Forget It.

*Maybe elephants never forget, but humans
do—and it's not such a bad thing.*

....

An article in *Scientific American** describes a time in 1999 when Jenny, a resident elephant at The Elephant Sanctuary in Hohenwald, Tennessee, was introduced to another elephant, a newcomer named Shirley. The elephants were so enthusiastic at their meeting that it prompted the sanctuary founder to research Shirley's background more thoroughly. As it turned out, the two elephants knew each other from a circus where they had performed together for a few months— 23 years earlier.

Maybe elephants never forget, but humans do. One of the more interesting—and annoying—aspects of human life is how we experience memory. While a few people in the world have Highly Superior Autobiographical Memory, or HSAM, it's rare. For the rest of us, it's a crap shoot—a special song from our youth can open a flood of vivid recollections, while other times, we can't recall what we ate for breakfast.

Remember all those chemistry, algebra and biology facts and formulas we had to learn in middle school and high school? It's astounding how many hours of our lives we spent ingesting all that stuff, only to regurgitate it for the final exam and then forget pretty much all of it for the rest of our lives. Seems like an awful lot of work for not much payback.

In contrast, consider what Eben Alexander, M.D. describes in his book, *Proof of Heaven: A Neurosurgeon's Journey into the Afterlife.* Alexander (a scientific thinker, not a religious man) had a near-death experience and lay in a coma for a week after succumbing to a rare illness. He had no brain activity during this time, yet emerged from the coma with memories of a beautiful, heaven-like place. What I find most intriguing about his description of heaven was that there, he only had to wonder about something—even a deep mystery of The Universe—and he would instantly, effortlessly understand it.

Maybe that's the way it is in heaven, but here on Earth,we have to study hard to understand and remember challenging topics. And only significant personal events remain strong in our memories, while most day-to-day details seem to get lost in the shuffle of daily routines and busyness. I only remember a handful of faint images from childhood. And don't even ask me where I was or what I was doing for much of my twenties, but I must have been doing something because I made it to my thirties. It seems as though humans are designed to forget things. But maybe it's not such a bad thing.

Consider this: with our faulty human memory, we do dumb, frustrating things like misplace our car keys, forget our own kids' names, and lose our entire recollection of anything we studied in school. But the flip side is, we also get to re-experience movies and books we loved the first time around; we know what's going to happen, but we can experience them again for the sheer enjoyment. We can do that because we forget the details.

And painful life events? Those memories fade, too—fortunately. Could you imagine how painful it would be, for example, to continually re-live the intensity of a loved one's death every time we thought about them? We can take comfort knowing that over time, we will forget the feeling of the initial loss while retaining the happy memories.

So, because we aren't like elephants, we can choose which events of our lives to revisit and cherish—and which ones to let slide away in the river of forgotten memories . . . like high school physics, for one.

* Ritchie, James, "Fact or Fiction?: Elephants Never Forget," Scientific American, January 12, 2009, https://www.scientificamerican.com/article/elephants-never-forget/

When You Say No,
You're Saying Yes

The secret superpower of "No"

....

Think about the last time you said "No" to something—it could have been a literal no, like a reply to a lunch meeting, or a figurative no, like thinking to yourself, *No, tonight I will not binge-watch Netflix while binge-eating donuts.*

Consider this: there's a flip side to "No." When you say no to something, you are also saying yes to something else; you're prioritizing what's most important to you and deciding how you are going to spend your finite time and energy. For example, saying no to the meeting could mean saying yes to an extra hour in your day to spend with your kids, and saying no to the binge night could mean saying yes to the gym—and better health.

There are many flavors of no, like finally saying no to those friends who are always asking for favors. Or declining your thirteenth invite this month to a friend's kid's birthday party. With this kind of no, you're saying yes to reclaiming and honoring your time.

If you say no to your family or society's expectations, you're saying yes to living your truth. The same goes for saying no to relationships, jobs, living spaces or other life situations that don't suit you anymore, or perhaps never did.

Saying no to buying new stuff you don't need means saying yes to a healthier financial life. Saying no to excess physical objects, clutter and things you don't use means saying yes to a calmer, clutter-free home and mind.

The benefits of "no" are obvious, but we don't always say it when we should. Why? There are a ton of reasons, but often, it boils down to fear—fear of people's reactions, fear of change, but most of all, fear of the unknown.

I learned something great about this from Kyle Cease, a former comedian who now does transformational comedy. He says that when we cut something out of our life, we can measure what we're losing but we can't measure what we may gain. And what we gain may be much bigger than anything we could have imagined.

You might be facing a no; maybe it's a big no or a small no. But whatever it is, it'll be easier to embrace that tiny, yet powerful word "no" when you consider the possible "yeses" behind it.

When I said "No" to my marriage, it was a huge, difficult "No." I could definitely measure all the things I had to lose—the house I'd built with my husband, our long history, our friends, my dream of a great marriage, and much more. But it became easier when I began to imagine the things I would also be saying yes to. And I'm thrilled to say that Cease was right—ultimately, what I gained by getting divorced was greater than anything I could have envisioned.

The next time you say no, think about what you're saying yes to—does it reflect who you truly are or want to be? And if you find it hard to say no, even when you know you should, think about all the "yeses" that lie waiting for you—and all the ones you can't even yet imagine.

Eat That Frog? Maybe Not.

*A journey of a thousand miles
can begin with a tiny hop.*

....

There's a philosophy of time management that supports "eating that frog" first thing in the morning. It means that if you tackle your biggest, most dreaded, most procrastination-worthy task and get it done, you can go through the rest of the day knowing that the worst is over and it's all downhill from there (in a good way). But there's a problem with this approach: if you tackle your biggest task first, you may never get to any of the other ones. Or your "frog task" may seem so overwhelming or discouraging that you can't figure out where to begin, which only makes you feel completely unproductive when the clock keeps ticking and you still have a billion other things to do.

Yes, there are times when you should grab that figurative frog and bite its head off, but there's another option. It's counterintuitive to the frog approach, but it's often the better choice:

Start smallest.

I read some investment advice once, given to a newly married couple who had many bills and debts. They had been following the common advice of the "frog" variety—pay off the largest first—but they were having a tough time with it; though they were slowly chipping away at it, they were still far from paying it off. They felt discouraged, especially knowing that once they paid off that huge debt, they still had the next-largest debt lined up, waiting behind it.

Their adviser had an unexpected suggestion: pay off the *smallest* bill first. They actually had enough money to do that right away, and they did. With that done easily, they had the satisfaction of checking one goal off their list. And guess what? Their excitement at doing so created the forward momentum they needed to pay off their next-smallest bill and their next. They still had to pay off their largest, but once they did, they could celebrate with the knowledge that it would be their last.

Sometimes when you face a new project, challenging endeavor, or overwhelming to-do list, you've got to eat a big frog. However, starting with the smallest tadpole is often a better approach.

I like what legendary tennis player Arthur Ashe said: "Start where you are. Use what you have. Do what you can." I'm not sure exactly what he was referring to when he said it, but it's great to remember when you're feeling overwhelmed.

Start anywhere . . . with anything. And if it's not enough, you can always begin again. Just do *something*.

Black Friday and
The Wizard of Oz

*Sometimes we need things.
Often, we already have them.*

....

Thanksgiving in the United States is typically followed by four days of shopping mania that includes Black Friday, Small Business Saturday and Cyber Monday. Some years, stores have even opened on Thanksgiving Day at 5 p.m. (supposedly so everyone could run out and shop, fueled by their turkey dinner) and stayed open until 1 or 2 a.m. on Black Friday, making it a full five days of orgasmic consumer hysteria.

Last Thanksgiving, my e-mail inbox was packed with "Don't miss these deals!" emails from all sorts of businesses. These ranged from clothing and furniture stores to other businesses, including a local theater and yoga studio that likely felt they had to jump on the bandwagon to stay competitive. I love saving money, so I grabbed a couple of great deals on things I was planning to buy anyway—a yoga class card, and a few embroidery designs I'd had on my wish list for months.

So, I saved on a couple of things I really wanted, but I also saw how tempting it can be to fall into the trap of FOMO (Fear of Missing Out). As I deleted each email, I had to pause and say, "Do I really need these clothes? This car? That furniture? That online course? Would I have bought this anyway, even if it wasn't a deal?" It reminded me of things I'd bought in years past and have yet to use—notably, a few online courses I've never logged into (or abandoned before I finished) and books in my bookcase I've bought and not yet read.

Remember *The Wizard of Oz*? Dorothy and her friends go on a great journey to find The Tin Man's heart, The Scarecrow's brains, The Lion's courage, and a way for Dorothy to get home. But when they finally meet "the great and powerful Oz," they learn that they already had, all along, the things they thought they needed. Similarly, if we look around,we can find many things we already have but never or barely use, such as:

- Workout equipment
- Gym memberships
- Gift certificates and online coupons
- Books
- Clothing
- Online courses
- Subscriptions to magazines and cable channels

Maybe you have some of these? Be honest.

The days after Thanksgiving can be a great time to snag great deals for ourselves and our homes, and gifts for our loved ones. And it's also an opportunity to remind ourselves of all the abundance we already have. Best yet, we don't have to journey to Oz dodging an evil witch and flying monkeys to find awesome stuff—we probably have a lot of it already, in our own homes and lives.

If you score some great post-Thanksgiving deals, awesome! But don't forget the stuff you already have. Read the books, log into the courses, dust off that exercise equipment and pick up those forgotten projects.

Like to save money? You'll save 100% when you don't buy anything at all. Use what you already have; maybe you don't need more.

Motivation Just Got Real

*The #1 thing that'll help you light
a fire under your own ass*

....

Ialways have a thousand things to do. I organize it all—
personal and professional to-dos, long-range goals, shoot-
for-the-stars dreams and lists—in a paper planner and digi-
tal list maker (thank you, Planner Pad and Trello). But for a
long time, I was organizing the hell out of my weeks and not
actually getting much *done*. It was then that I remembered
something I'd heard lots of motivational gurus talk about—
the "why."

Simon Sinek has created an entire empire around "why"—
he wrote the books *Start With Why* and *Find Your Why* and
also has a viral *TED Talk* video on the topic. Sinek delves
into the "whys" on a large scale—how a sense of purpose
and meaning relates to corporate missions, people's careers,
and life paths. But if you just want to get motivated and don't
care to spend hours of your life exploring the limbic brain,
the neocortex, and all the thrilling wonders of the biology of
human decision-making (which you will have to do if you
absorb all of Sinek's material), you can just take a cue from
his book titles.

If you have to get certain things done (and I'm assuming
these are things you must do, or you wouldn't do them),
you'll get better at doing them if you take a few minutes to
think about *why* you want to get them done. And be honest.
Life coach and author Mel Robbins touched on this in her
own impressive *TED Talk*, "How to Stop Screwing Yourself
Over." Robbins says, for example, that if you tell yourself you
want to lose weight and get in shape to "be healthy," that

motivation will likely last all of 24 hours. However, if your motivation is to finally get a girlfriend/boyfriend and get laid, that's the kind of brutal self-honesty that will get you into your gym clothes and out of the house for a run when it's cold and dark and your warm bed beckons you to never, ever leave.

Now, when I plan my week, I connect a motivator to as many things as I can—it makes a huge difference. For example, writing a chapter gets me one step closer to writing a whole book. Or having lunch with a friend is a way I can build a relationship I value. Or doing my workout will feel great and help prevent me from becoming a fat, old, unhealthy fart. And honestly, sometimes the biggest motivator is just that I'm tired of seeing that *thing* in my planner, undone week after week, and I just want to get it out of my life. It's strangely effective, at least for me.

Find what motivates you, and be honest about it. Now go get shit done.

Send the Damn Card

....

I once attended a 10-day training program at Kripalu Center for Yoga & Health with a wonderful group of women. It was fall, summer temperatures were cooling, and the foliage in the Berkshires provided a beautiful backdrop for our program and for our budding new friendships with each other.

I kept in touch with a few of those women and, a couple of months later, I sent Christmas cards to them along with my usual cards to close friends and family. There was one woman from the program whom I'd liked, but I waffled back and forth about sending her a card—we hadn't really been close, but she was nice enough. Ultimately, I included her in my mailing; I had a few extra cards and, well, *What the hell,* I thought. *Why not?*

The next year I ran into her again at the yoga center and she thanked me profusely for the card (which I'd long forgotten). As it turned out, the year I'd met her, she had left a 30-something-year-old marriage, and all of her in-laws, friends and family had shunned her for it. I'd had no idea. That Christmas she received no holiday invites, phone calls, or greetings of any kind—except my card. Though she'd spent the holiday alone, my card reminded her that *someone* still cared about her.

You never know what your small gesture of kindness might mean to someone. So mail the card. Send the text. Tell a stranger you like their pants. If you're on the fence, go ahead. Do it.

Empty That Cup
Before You Fill It Up

Want cool stuff? Make room for it first.

....

The first day of a new year is a common time for many of us to make big plans. A new year—especially a "big" one like a new decade or millennium—promises a fresh start, an inspired new beginning, and all kinds of auspicious and amazing stuff. People generally get very excited about this; resolutions are made, goals are set, and proclamations of "This is the Year!" are announced to friends, family and Facebook.

There's just one thing—we have to let go of old stuff to make room for new stuff. There's a popular martial arts tale about "emptying your cup," where a Zen master keeps filling the teacup of an opinionated wisdom-seeker until tea is overflowing all over the place (no doubt creating a burn hazard and huge mess). The idea is, if you are too full of old thoughts, teachings, or ideas, you've got no room left for any more, and you must empty your cup before you can accept new knowledge.

I believe this applies not just to philosophies or wisdom, but to new things of every kind; the act of consciously vacating space creates a vacuum that helps attract what we want in its place. So as part of a personal, annual New Year's Day ritual, I get rid of (donate or give away) one physical item from my living space (bonus points for choosing something that's been annoying me for so long I hardly see it anymore). It symbolizes "emptying my cup" and creating room for all the new, better-than-last-year stuff I actively welcome into my life in the coming year.

On the first day of the year, or any time you want to create change, I invite you to do the same; get rid of something. Doesn't matter what it is—it can be big or small—because it's not the size of the object but the act of setting it free that will create an energy shift. Because all that great shit you want needs somewhere to go. Make space for it now.

Be a Quitter

....

I did a wonderful thing last week: I fired a client. She had hired me for a small, low-budget freelance editing job that was supposed to be a quick transaction and take maybe an hour of my time. Easy, right? I finished the job and delivered a high-quality piece of writing that was everything she had asked for. *Job complete*, I thought.

Then the fun started. She asked for a revision and sent more text to add (neither of which was included in our agreement). And then she asked for another revision, and another. And all the while, her requests (through an online messaging system) were getting increasingly cryptic and difficult to understand to the point where, honestly, I was questioning her sanity. In just a few days, the job had already occupied too much of my time and too many of my thoughts. The solution became clear: end it.

She was upset when I canceled the job, even though I did so very professionally, and I had already delivered a product and services that had far exceeded our agreement. And just that quickly, I was free—free to direct my brain power, life energy and thoughts in more productive directions, and free of an energy vampire who was probably never going to be satisfied. Yes, I quit—and it was the right thing to do.

In life, business and sports, there's a popular stigma about quitting. "Quitters" are criticized for being lazy, giving up easily, and not having the balls, grit, stamina or perseverance to finish what they start. The message is clear: *Don't give up! Don't be a quitter like the other guy! Success could be right around the corner!*

That's often true. But other times, the desired result (pleasing a client, finishing a project, reaching a goal, etc.) will always remain just out of reach, like that proverbial carrot dangling from a stick. Or maybe circumstances have changed, and the direction you're going in is no longer a good one. Sometimes, yes, the right thing to do is to keep pushing ahead, but sometimes, the best thing to do is quit. Especially when quitting something means gaining something else—like self-respect, dignity, money and/or time.

Stick it out or quit? The best course of action isn't always obvious, especially when you're trying to decide whether to stay in or get out of something big like a marriage, relationship, job or career; dilemmas like these can give us sleepless nights and calloused brains as we desperately try to decide what to do. (And if you need help deciding, you might like *The Dip: A Little Book That Teaches You When to Quit (and When to Stick)* by Seth Godin.)

Sometimes, we need to pull on our big girl or big boy pants and stick shit out, keep plugging away, and finish what we start, because the hard stuff often brings us to the good stuff, and sometimes the journey itself has purpose. But other times, the best thing we can do is quit. That's when quitting is far from weak; it's empowering.

Everything Happens for a Reason . . . and Other Lies

Have you ever read someone's social media post about a personal challenge or tragedy? Among the supportive "I'm sorry" responses, eventually there will be at least one person who writes, "Everything happens for a reason."

They mean well. If we're in the midst of some huge life challenge—a death, divorce, illness, or other sucky life event, the rationale "Everything happens for a reason," from the lips of a caring friend, has the power to pop us out of our self-focused bubble of sorrow. The rationale stops us long enough to feel a little hope or see just a bit beyond the situation. Or if we're reflecting on that sucky life event years after it happened, we can trace our paths backward, see how some good things came out of that crappy thing, and tell ourselves, "Everything happens for a reason."

I'm not going to be a total Debbie Downer and say that the "Everything happens for a reason" notion is total bullshit; maybe it's not. Honestly, I really would like to believe it's true, because it would help make sense of many of life's conundrums (like global warming, war, or why women swoon over Christian Bale). But I also think we humans have the *need* to assign meaning to the shitstorms of life, because if we feel there is some deeper meaning or ultimate purpose, it makes everything easier to bear.

I once interviewed a cancer survivor for an article I was writing. He said his big takeaway from the whole experience of diagnosis, chemotherapy, radiation and remission was, "God writes in letters too large for us to read." And when I lost a job I loved due to a massive corporate reorganization, all seemed very bleak until I landed an even better job two weeks later. Looking back, I could say I may never have landed the second job if I hadn't lost the first. In cases like those, we can rationalize the good in the bad, and doing so makes everything feel better.

Conversely, we can make situations *more* difficult when we assign them meaning, especially when we're facing a tough decision or don't want to face the truth. I know—I've done it, and I've watched others do it, too. A friend of mine was having some big relationship issues with his girlfriend. The relationship had run its course and the obvious solution was to break it off, but he wouldn't. Why? Because a couple of years previous, when he was single and lonely (and likely dying to get laid on a regular basis), he'd prayed for a girlfriend. And God, he believed, had delivered her to him. "How can I break up with Margaret when God gave her to me?" he said. Had God literally answered his prayer and delivered Margaret? Well, I can't speak for God. But I can tell you that my friend spent several more months miserable, trying to resuscitate an already-dead relationship because of the meaning he'd assigned to it.

No matter what choices we make or circumstances that befall us in life, painful shit will happen. And when it does, there will inevitably be someone sending you internet memes that say, "Everything happens for a reason" on soft-focus sunset backgrounds. Or, worse yet, they may send you video links to Rascal Flatts singing "Bless the Broken Road." But the truth is, we can find meaning in *any* possible outcome if we look hard enough.

Does everything *really* happen for a reason? Maybe it does. But we should also embrace the possibility that it doesn't. And if that's the case, don't despair, because we still have the option to assign our own meaning to a situation. And since we have that freedom, we might as well make as many things as we can mean something awesome.

Feeling Off-Kilter?
Maybe It's Time to Filter.

Make social media your bitch,
not the other way around.

....

There are a ton of articles and commentaries on the internet about the evils of social media and cell phones. I promise that this won't be another one.

Social media—like many technologies—has value. To me, Facebook is great for staying up to date on the daily life events of far-flung friends. For example, I have a close Australian friend who posts about her son's basketball games and the hot weather (when it's freezing cold here in the United States). I love reading about those little day-to-day nuggets of life that are the stuff of Facebook posts but probably wouldn't be important enough for her to mention in a video chat. I also participate in a number of Facebook groups, and from them, I've learned a ton of useful things about business and my hobbies.

However, like many things, social media can be "good" or "bad" depending on how we use it and how we let it influence our daily life. Here are two common reasons people cite for why social media is "bad":

It invites comparison.

People share quick glimpses of their lives on social media, and it's usually the best stuff. It's easy to feel envious when you see mostly pictures of adorable cats, smiling children, sparkling-clean houses, and dream vacations. People typically don't share posts of their trips to the bathroom, laundry folding or commuting. If they did, we'd know that just about everyone's life has moments that are as mundane as ours.

It's a potentially endless time suck.

It happens to everyone—you pick up your phone to check an email and think, "I'll just see what's happening on Facebook or Instagram first." Next thing you know, it's 20 minutes later, you're watching videos of peppermint brownie recipes, dancing cats or "10 Most Dangerous Fire Rescues" and you still haven't checked that e-mail. (The "time suck" factor alone is why I stopped playing Words With Friends.)

One more reason I've never actually read about, but I think is the most important:

It's a chaotic assault on the senses.

Where will you see those peppermint brownie recipes, dancing cats or "10 Most Dangerous Fire Rescues"—all lumped together with inspirational memes, friend requests— and other stuff you might actually be interested in? Social media, that's where. The human brain probably wasn't designed for the massive mental shifts necessary to process such eclectic onslaughts of information. In a single session with our cell phone, we're typically exposed to information ranging from simple and soothing to complex and anxiety-provoking, and we don't know what to expect or when to expect it. I think it exhausts the brain, at least on some primal level.

Social media isn't the enemy, though—if we use it wisely. Think about a knife—it can be used to cut vegetables into a delicious salad, or it can be used to stab someone. Technology is the same way; used wisely, as a tool, it can serve or control us—our choice.

I've been downsizing many areas of my life, my social media and cell phone use included. I recently installed an app on my phone that limits how much time I spend per day on Facebook (my biggest social media time waster). After 15 minutes, it gives me a warning, and an option to ignore it. Sometimes, I do ignore it—for long enough to finish reading a good article or inspiring post. But most of the time, I shut it off. And you know what? It's been a great tool for refining my focus; if I know I only have 15 minutes a day to spend on Facebook, I'm much more motivated to filter out the posts that are time and energy wasters, and head straight for the meaningful posts—things that educate, motivate, inspire or inform me, or that help me feel more connected to special people. And that leaves much more time for real life.

We do not have unlimited time, but we have unlimited ways to use it. May you use your time—on or off social media—in ways that best serve you.

Got Haters? Then You're Doing Something Right.

There are seven and a half billion people in the world, and we could group them into many different categories. Today, we'll divide people into two groups: those who *do* the things they really want to do in life, and those who *want to* do things but don't.

People in the latter group invent all sorts of excuses for why they're not doing the things they want to do or know they should, and they hate those who are doing—or attempting to do—those things. The haters are easy to identify—they're the ones who'll criticize you for your success. If you've done something like lose weight, quit smoking, or launch a successful business, I bet you've encountered at least a few.

I recently listened to an interview with super-successful businessperson and author Dean Graziosi. He described how one of his early rental properties had a lawn so large that it would take him an entire day—hours of sweaty, exhausting work—to mow and landscape. Finally, Graziosi realized that it would be a much smarter investment of his time and money to hire a local teen to do the yard work, freeing up Graziosi to complete other, more profitable business tasks that same day.

Graziosi's father—a proud blue-collar worker—showed up at the property one day while the teen was mowing the lawn. He became infuriated with Graziosi, saying that his hiring a laborer made him "too big for his britches," and drove off in a huff, sending gravel flying all over the side of his son's car. It was then, Graziosi said, that he knew he was doing something right because it had triggered such a strong reaction from his father.

I was once dealt a similar remark from one of the guest instructors of a yoga dance teacher training I attended. During the program, I joyfully shared many things with my enthusiastic fellow students, including a dance sequence I'd created, and an impromptu martial arts demonstration. One afternoon, when there weren't many of the others within earshot, the instructor sarcastically purred in my direction, "Oh, Wendy's good at *evvverything*."

Ironically, it was later in that training that another student's visiting eight-year-old daughter unknowingly described my encounter with the instructor: "My teacher said that when you point your finger at someone, you're really pointing three fingers back at yourself."

Think about the last time someone offered up a cutting remark, tried to discourage you, or minimized your skills or talent. Chances are, the issue wasn't really about you doing something wrong—it was about them getting tweaked because you were doing something right.

Dumbass things you may hear when you're doing something right:

- "You're too big for your britches!"
- "Oh, thousands of people have failed at that. Remember your Aunt Bertha?"
- "Oh, so you think you're better than the rest of us?"
- "Aren't you too [young/old/black/white/rich/poor/female/male] for that?"
- "Yeah, you're doing great today, but . . ."
- "But the economy is so bad right now. In fact, they say a recession is coming!"

When you do something well, your success will inspire and motivate like-minded doers. But your success will also shine a light on the shortcomings and excuses of haters and their failure to give their own dreams a chance. When they give you shit for being the best version of your awesome self, don't feel obligated to shrink because of their insecurities. Instead, see their negativity as confirmation that you're doing something right. And keep right on doing it.

Don't Fight the Flow

....

Once upon a time, I was busting my ass trying to get into a school program for a particular medical career. I had fulfilled all the requirements, taken all the prerequisite courses (and gotten straight As), provided reference letters, and was more than qualified. But they had a two-year waiting list, with special admissions given to only a lucky few. I wasn't one of them.

I knew quite a few people working in the field who had already gone through the program and were familiar with the school staff. "Talk to so-and-so," they said. I did. "Do such-and-such," they said. I did. But still, I couldn't leverage admission into the next class, and I was eager to get on with it, dammit!

When I heard through the grapevine that there were several vacancies in the class that was about to start, I showed up on the first day, hoping that my initiative would make an impression about how serious I was, and I would catch a break. My mission was clear: Push! Make it happen! Fight for what you want! But I *still* couldn't get in; no one with authority would budge.

Exasperated, I vented my frustration with a friend who wisely shared a different viewpoint: Chill out, girl. Maybe it's not meant to happen, at least not now.

You see, we can't always make stuff happen the way we want; we have to co-create with The Universe (or whatever you want to call it, him, her or them). It's a creation partnership: you do everything you can, and The Big U will do everything *it* can. But sometimes, even when we *do* and *do* and *do* . . . shit doesn't happen—even shit we want very much. It can feel like we're in a rowboat, furiously rowing, but never moving. Because no matter how hard you work, if

The Universe isn't working with you, you won't get anywhere.

It's at times like these, I learned, that we must let go of the damn oars, take note of which direction we're paddling (usually upstream), and turn our boat around. When I finally turned my figurative boat downstream, guess what happened? I got a great job offer in a completely different field that I loved even more.

I did finally get the news I'd been waiting to hear—that I'd secured a spot in the next class. But by then, two years had passed, I was happy in my job, and glad I hadn't had to go back to school to get the position.

The next time you're paddling like crazy but the scenery isn't changing, take note of where your boat is pointed. Maybe it's time to lift your oars out of the water, drift a bit, and see where the current takes you.

Pulling Up

*Discovering the hidden
power in cycling and life*

....

I'm in my 50s and learning to ride a bike. I mean, I've been
riding bikes since I was a kid, and I did some pretty regular mountain biking 25 years ago, but this is the first time
I've *really* learned how to ride. Let me explain.

My boyfriend introduced me to spin fitness classes—you
know, where you ride a stationary bike in a darkened, music-
filled room with other people, and you all ride nowhere
together but it's a great workout. He'd been a spin class and
cycling enthusiast before we met, and he advised me early on
that one *had* to have clip-in shoes if one was serious about
either of those endeavors. I'd get much more power out of
each pedal stroke, he said, with my foot secured to the pedal.

I had my doubts; sticking my shoes to the pedals of any
bike sounded about as safe as walking a tightrope with my
feet duct-taped to 10-pound dumbbells. But once I tried the
special shoes in spin class (and embraced waddling like a
duck when I walked in them), I realized that my boyfriend
was right. Apparently, soft sneaker soles absorb a lot of the
power you're trying to transfer to the pedal. What's more,
with your feet clipped in, you power your bike not just by
pushing *down* on the pedals but also pulling *up*.

A few weeks ago, we both started cycling again—on *real*
bikes. Which meant I had to re-learn how to ride a bike with
those damn clip shoes. The actual riding part was easy—it
was, well, like riding a bike. But overcoming the fear of
clipping in and navigating bike path walkers, runners, roll-
erbladers and other cyclists—all with your feet glued to the

pedals—plus learning to unclip and stop for cars at intersections without tipping over and breaking your ass on the pavement—that was tough. They call them "SPD" clips (an acronym for Shimano Pedaling Dynamics) but at first, they felt So Pointless and Dumb, and when I fell, I felt like Such a Profound Doofus.

But with a better pair of shoes and some practice, I've come to love this kind of cycling. On a real bike, the foot/pedal connection with clip shoes is even more powerful than on a spin bike. Seriously, it's amazing; you can propel yourself forward not just with the downstroke of the pedal, but the upstroke too.* Now I think SPD should stand for Super-Powered and Deadly, because when you power your upstroke, it's no longer just a useless rest between the "real" downstroke moments, but an addition to them.

All of this got me thinking about many things (and on long rides, you have lots of time to think). Mostly, I thought about how many times I've ridden a bike before and never knew there was a better way to do it, and how I might find hidden sources of power in other areas of life.

The human journey has its own upstrokes and downstrokes—sometimes we call them hills and valleys. What if we were to find the power in the upstrokes of life as well as the downstrokes? If we did, could each of us double our productivity, significance, or sense of well-being? I haven't figured it out yet, but the possibilities are mind-blowing. Maybe the answer lies right around the next bend.

* Die-hard cyclists break it down into the downstroke, backstroke, upstroke and overstroke, but that's too much for me to think about right now.

More is Less

A little carry-on taught me a big lesson.

....

I wanted to back out, but I couldn't. There was no way I was going to fit all the things I needed for seven days in a carry-on. But I'd already promised, so I had to find a way.

When I'd planned a week-long tropical vacation with a friend of mine, she proposed that we only take carry-on suitcases—one each—and thus avoid the extra time and hassle of baggage claim. "Sure," I said, not fully thinking it through.

When it was time to pack, I couldn't fit everything I planned to bring, but I had to do it, somehow. So I took a huge mental step back and reassessed everything—every last item—I had been planning to pack. Did I *really* need to bring the full-size moisturizer? No, just what I needed for seven days. Did I *really* need to bring the full-size makeup brushes? No, the travel set would do just fine. Did I *really* need to bring all the items of clothing I was bringing "just in case" something got wet or dirty, or could I probably get by re-wearing things or washing them, if need be? What essentials could I buy when I got to our destination? And on it went.

Then I re-packed, and an interesting thing happened; I actually had *extra* room in my carry-on bag. So I fit in another dress and pair of flip-flops—luxury items, I thought.

We had a wonderful time on our vacation, but one of the most memorable parts of the trip, for me, was after I returned home. When I unpacked my little suitcase, I separated the items I'd used from those I hadn't and was shocked at what I saw: *two-thirds* of the items I'd brought hadn't been used or worn—including the bonus dress and flip-flops.

Ever since that vacation, I look at my "needs" differently,

and not just when packing for a trip. How many shirts do I *really* need in my closet? How many towels do I *really* use in a week? How many multiples of something must I *really* store in my house? The answer is, usually: *a lot less than I thought*. Just as I had felt liberated wheeling my little carry-on through the airport, thinking, *everything I need for the whole week is right here*, minimizing my possessions makes me feel empowered, not deprived.

We don't need all the things we often think we do. And that's a great life lesson to carry on.

Try Something You Hate

You might like it, in spite of yourself.

....

A good friend once invited me to an exhibit about Princess Diana. It featured Diana's personal belongings, pictures and home videos, and artifacts that honored her life from childhood through adulthood. The grand finale of the exhibit was an entire hall of Diana's glamorous clothing—her ball gowns and yes, *that* wedding dress. From what my friend described, the exhibit promised to be a practically orgasmic, not-to-be-missed tribute to the woman who had risen from humble, obscure beginnings to become the iconic Princess of Wales.

There was just one problem: I hated Princess Diana. But I liked my friend more than I hated Princess Diana, so I reluctantly agreed to go. I figured I'd be stifling yawns and checking my watch the entire time, but a funny thing happened once we started walking through the exhibit; I got interested—*really* interested.

I've always hated celebrity gossip, so that's probably why I had decided, way back when the tabloids liked to talk about her, that I didn't like Princess Diana. But the Diana honored in the exhibit was the *real* Diana, not the stuff of tabloid trash.

My friend and I stayed more than two and a half hours, until the exhibit closed and the security guards shooed us out and locked the doors. And in that time, I learned all I had ignored about Princess Diana while she was alive: that she had been an athletic child talented in music, dance and sports; that her engagement and marriage to Prince Charles had thrust her into both the Royal Family and the international spotlight; that she had done significant charity work for children and youth; that she had advocated tirelessly for those affected by HIV/AIDS, mental illness, disease, and landmines. And she had done it all with a quiet, endearing elegance distinctly her own.

The Princess Diana exhibit inspired me to say, "Hell, yeah!" to just about anything friends have invited me to since. It's led to some amazing experiences, including running an obstacle course on sand dunes, another exhibit about The Beatles, four Marc Cohn* concerts in four years, and a performance by Meat Loaf. And you know what? I've liked everything except the Meat Loaf concert. But even that gave me insight into the friend who invited me to see it, and that alone was worth it.

From the Diana exhibit, I learned all about an iconic person in history. More importantly, I learned that when you try something new, you might just be surprised—about your "likes," your friends, and the world outside your small circle of preferences.

Marc Cohn is the guy who won a Grammy for "Walking in Memphis." See him live if you ever get the chance; he's an incredibly funny and entertaining performer.

Riding Through Chaos

....

You're in the passenger seat of a car that's driving down a road, when suddenly the driver swerves to miss a pothole. What do you do? Most of us instinctively reach out and grab something stable, like the door handle. If you're already buckled in, it's not actually going to do much, but it makes you feel better. It's a reflexive action—grabbing on to something that's still when all else around you is shifting.

I'm reminded of a quote I once saw about how "Peace" doesn't mean there is no noise, trouble or hard work. Rather, it means that you can be in the midst of those things and still be calm in your heart. When it feels like everything around me is chaotic and the world is going to shit, I know I can be calm in my heart if I make a conscious effort to reach for that figurative door handle.

If you're struggling to stay peaceful in the midst of chaos, you might try two things that work well for me:

Step back—way back.

In the United States, the end of May 2020 was a time of deep racial tension, pain and disorder in many communities. Also at this time, SpaceX's Dragon shuttle left Earth carrying NASA astronauts Robert Behnken and Douglas Hurley. The next day, they joined NASA astronaut Chris Cassidy and Russian cosmonauts Anatoli Ivanishin and Ivan Vagner at the International Space Station, then in orbit above China's border with Mongolia. If we can have that kind of global cooperation in space, surely we must be able to accomplish that within our countries and communities.

A common realization among astronauts is their appreciation of the fragile beauty of our planet as viewed from afar, and their desire for others to explore space as they have. If they could, life on Earth "would be vastly different," they say.* In space it's quiet, you have beautiful views, and everyone gets along. I don't know this from personal experience, but the next best thing is watching videos from space. (If you have a few minutes, search *YouTube* for Commander Chris Hadfield's hauntingly beautiful rendition of the song "Space Oddity," recorded during a stay on the International Space Station. I dare you to watch that and *not* feel more peaceful and reflective.)

Get close—very close.

Nature is an incredible stabilizer; it keeps on doing its thing no matter what the stupid humans around it are doing. If I'm feeling off-center, I get outside if I can. Sometimes I'll observe a leaf—a single leaf. I look closely at its veins, its color, its structure, and I see how there's an entire world within it, happily going on about its business whether I notice or not.

I look just as closely at my bunny Nelson's fur. I marvel at his long eyelashes, and how every hair in his coat has its own beautiful pattern of ombre color. I feel his teeth grinding with happiness when he's held, and I laugh at the unbridled joy he gets from a tiny treat. But I can only notice these things when I slow down and focus enough to see them.

I also find comfort in a Facebook friend's posts about the animals on her farm—the tortoises that amble out of their stall predictably at 7 a.m. and return for bed every night at 6 p.m.—old farts. And her chicken, Bowling Pin, who defends her favorite tree stump from any other chicken who dares try and share it with her. Like humans, they have their conflicts, but it's over after a few pecks.

No, we can't ignore the chaos around us—nor should we. But it's especially during trying times like these that we must take time to find our own "door handle" and hold on tight. Because it's only then that we will make it calmly through the bumpy ride.

Davenport, Christian, and Vitkovskaya, Julie, 50 Astronauts, In Their Own Words, The Washington Post, June 19, 2019.

Fill 'Er Up!

....

"I miss shopping," my friend said during the coronavirus lockdown, after weeks of not visiting her favorite stores for her usual recreational retail therapy. Though I don't love shopping as much as she does, I also had to cut down my shopping considerably, to mostly just grocery essentials.

We all had to shift our habits during the COVID-19 lockdowns, and it forced us to find new routines, create new ways to get things done, and reevaluate what's essential. During lockdown, I started cutting my boyfriend's hair every week, which he used to get done at the barber for twenty dollars a pop. He's loving it. This same guy also reevaluated his "need" for a gym membership, since he found that his home workouts were just as effective as his gym workouts, with the added benefits of clean, always-available equipment, a lack of "meatheads" in his workout space, and a 10-second walk to his workout instead of a 10-minute drive. He doesn't intend to ever return to the barber or re-join the gym—at a savings of almost $1,500 a year.

Another friend of mine sheepishly confessed that the social distancing rules gave her the perfect excuse to avoid toxic friends and family, and her mental health was never better. Lockdown forced her to reevaluate who she would spend her valuable time with, post-coronavirus. And when I needed storage shelves but couldn't find anything online without exorbitant shipping charges, I made my own from lumber I had in the garage. Now I'm inspired to make whatever else I need in the future; who wants overpriced particleboard crap, anyway?

Every New Year's, I deliberately get rid of something, to physically and metaphysically create a void for the upcoming year's new blessings. The coronavirus imposed such voids in all of our lives and forced us to give up many things. What's important to recognize, though, is that while we had no control over what we lost from our everyday lives, we have a choice in what we allow back. For the first time ever, on a global scale, it's not a matter of the glass being half empty or full—it's a matter of what we put in the glass.

The Global Reset

....

The COVID-19 pandemic of 2020 was tragic. Not only is the virus vicious, mysterious and pervasive, but it has far-reaching social, economic and emotional ripple effects we are still feeling. In some ways, though, it was also a wake-up call the world needed.

Don't get me wrong—the virus, and everything with it—sucks. For the thousands who died and the millions more who still mourn them, it especially sucks. For the thousands of "long-haulers" who are still feeling its long-term effects, it continues to suck. However, it took something of this magnitude to wake us up and shake us up, and that's not such a bad thing.

People are notoriously terrible at change, even when it's good for us. We know we shouldn't smoke, but we do. We know we should exercise, but we don't. We know we shouldn't be assholes to others, but we often are. As a society, we know we should preserve the Earth, give to charities, and be kind to our neighbors. However, we typically go through our days unconsciously doing all sorts of dumb shit instead of the stuff we know we should. We'd been sleepwalking through life, and it had been a luxury. COVID-19 woke us all the hell up—all over the world, at the same time.

Yes, we all saw the news stories—and maybe saw with our own eyes—people here and there gathering in crowds, going to church or not obeying orders to maintain a healthy social distance. But for the most part, people who otherwise would never actually do all the things they know they should were suddenly doing the right thing—practicing social distance, staying home, and wearing masks. Fear of death is an incredible motivator.

Many of us also reached out to neighbors, made and donated masks, volunteered our time, and generally became nicer human beings. We knew our lives didn't depend on doing those things, but we did them anyway, because we suddenly realized how vulnerable we are and how much we care about and need others.

Author James Fahy wrote, "Nothing unites humans like a common enemy," and COVID-19 proved to be a formidable foe.

It's tragic that it took something of that magnitude to wake us from our sleepwalk, but I prefer to remember the silver lining. What else but a worldwide pandemic would cause the kind of change that makes people stay home, sing to each other from balconies, and decrease car and air travel so much that air quality over large cities measurably improved?

When you've tried everything you know to solve a computer issue, sometimes the only thing that works is to just hit Ctrl-Alt-Delete and reset the whole damn machine. Similarly, COVID-19 forced everyone in the world to do a massive, simultaneous reboot—of our habits, our thoughts, and our mindsets. It's a positive shift that I hope goes viral.

Acknowledgments

....

I would like to extend my most sincere, heartfelt thanks to my readers, especially anyone who has ever written a letter, sent an email, or otherwise taken the time to express how my writing has impacted them.

To my friends who have supported my writing over the years and who eagerly anticipated each *Wendy Z Wednesday* essay, notably Chris, Diane, Kelly, Kevin, Krissy, Kristen, Linda, Mike, and Roxanne, thank you; I kept writing because you kept reading.

I would like to thank Maureen (Philp) Rogers, my eagle-eyed proofreader, editor and friend from my corporate days. May we always make others uneasy when we walk slowly, heads together, whispering and giggling.

Thank you Gina De Lise Rombley, for suggesting Stillwater River Publications.

Thank you Mom, Dad, and my brother Andy, for always encouraging and appreciating my writing. Jonathan and Jack, my nephews, I hope these reflections inspire you to live your best lives.

Thank you John Patrick Morgan and my 2020-2021 coaching circle (Alex, Christine, Danah, Denisa, Kelly-Ann, Michelle, Miquel, Moishe Dov, Sam and Winnie), for your feedback, unbridled honesty, and for daring me to dream big writing dreams.

Special thanks to Scott, for being my greatest cheerleader, supporter, and motivator. You are the wind in my sails. Everything I could say about you and us would fill another book.

Most of all, I thank the gift of writing for choosing me and for being a lifelong friend. And I thank that unknown place from where the words mysteriously flow.

Made in United States
North Haven, CT
10 April 2022

18100759R00050